NOW YOU CAN R

WILD ANIMALS

TEXT BY STEPHEN ATTMORE

ILLUSTRATED BY BOB HERSEY

BRIMAX BOOKS • NEWMARKET • ENGLAND

Here are some big wild animals. Look at the giraffe. What is it eating? A giraffe can see a long way. It is the tallest animal in the world. What a long neck! Zebras look like striped horses. They eat grass. They can smell other animals a long way away.

The elephants are having a shower. They suck up water in their trunks and spray it over their backs. An elephant's trunk is a very long nose. Look at the baby elephant standing between its mother's legs.

The lion is the king of wild animals. Lions live and hunt in a group called a pride. They kill and eat zebras and giraffes. Lion cubs have dark spots on their sides. Look at the cheetah running. It is the fastest animal on land. It can run at 70 mph.

These wild animals are hyenas. They howl when they are excited. The sound is like people laughing.

This is an anteater. Look at its long snout. It pushes its long, sticky tongue into ants' nests and eats the ants.

The hippopotamus is a big animal. Its name means ‘river horse’. Hippos stay in the water for most of the day. This keeps them cool. They come out onto the land at night to eat grass. Look for the small eyes on top of the hippo’s head.

A rhinoceros is a heavy creature. It eats leaves, twigs and grass. In the evening, rhinos roll in the mud beside a river. This helps them to cool down. Look at the two rhinos charging at each other.

These animals live in forests in North America. Look at the beaver. It uses its sharp teeth to chop down small trees. Beavers build dams across streams. The bear cub is climbing a tree. The animal with prickly spikes is a porcupine.

These animals live in woods in Europe. The female deer is eating twigs and buds. Look at the antlers on the head of the male deer. Each year they drop off and new ones grow. Look for the baby deer. The red foxes are stalking the deer. Look at their bushy tails.

Some wild animals live in trees. Look at the monkeys. They are eating fruit and leaves. They leap from tree to tree. Gorillas are much larger. When they walk they use their hands and their feet. When a gorilla is angry it hoots. It beats its chest with its hands.

Look at the squirrel. The long bushy tail helps it to balance on the branch. A squirrel's home is called a drey. Look for the bats hanging upside down. They sleep during the day and fly at night. They have thin skin between their long fingers. This is like a wing.

These wild animals live in Australia. Look for the baby kangaroo. It is peeping out of a pouch on its mother's tummy. Look at the kangaroos leaping. They have strong back legs.

Koalas live in trees. They feed at night on leaves and shoots. The baby koala is clinging to its mother's back. The duck-billed platypus lays eggs in a burrow. It has small ears and small eyes. Its bill is covered in skin and has nostrils at the end.

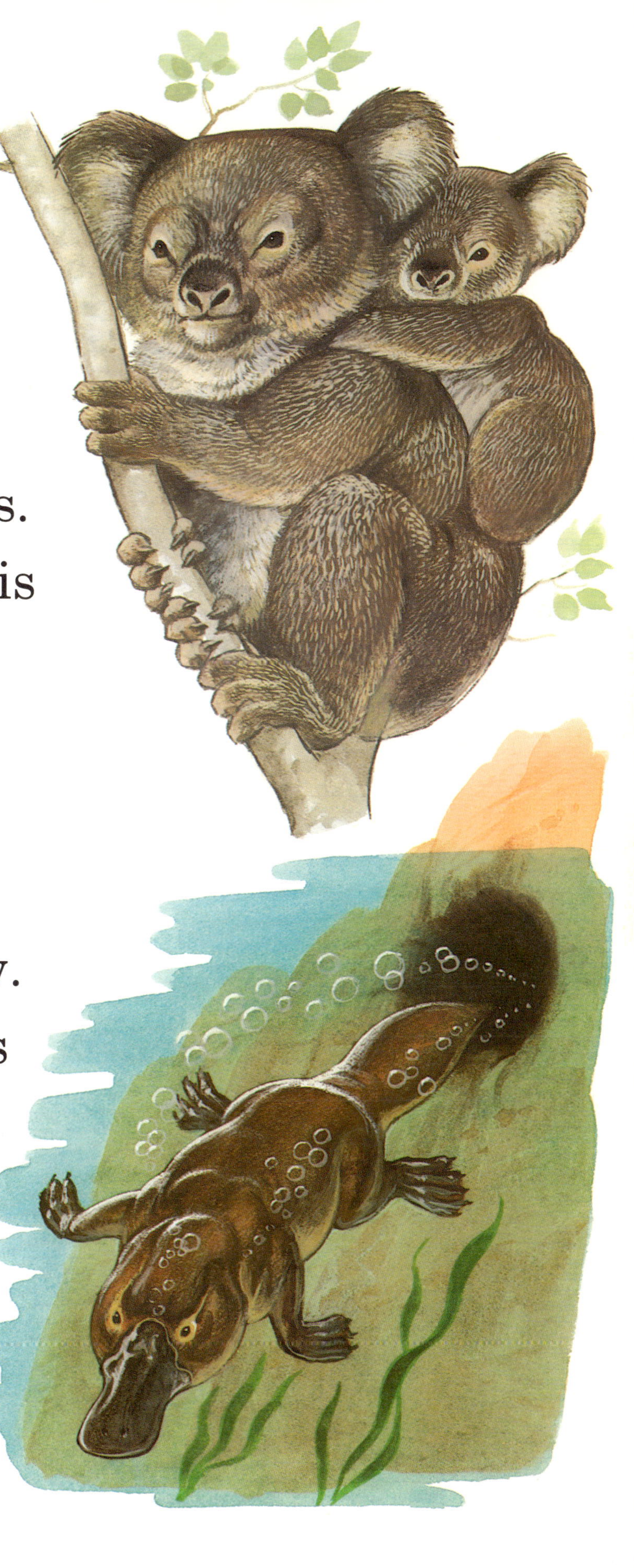

Animals need water and food. There is very little water or food in hot desert lands. Few animals live there. Camels travel long distances without stopping. They store water in their bodies. In a sandstorm they close their nostrils and eyes.

This small cat lives in a desert. Its feet have thick pads on the bottom. This makes it easier for the cat to move on sand. It rests during the day and hunts at night. The gazelle feeds on grass and roots. It can go without water for over a week. It runs very fast.

Some wild animals live in the mountains. The puma is leaping down on to a llama. Pumas are also called cougars. A snow leopard is following a yak. What long horns the yak has!

Chipmunks live in long tunnels. They carry food in their cheek pouches. They store nuts, seeds, fruit and berries to eat in winter. Look at the mountain goat on a high ledge. It feeds on grass.

Only a few animals live in the cold lands near the North and South poles. Look at the walruses. What long tusks! Did you know that walruses swim underwater on their backs? They break through the ice on the surface with their tusks.

This big white animal is a polar bear. It kills and eats seals. It has hairy soles on its feet. These stop it from sliding on the ice. Baby bears are born blind. They stay in a den with their mother until spring comes.

In this book you have read about many wild animals. Do you know where these wild animals live?

Buffalo

Tiger

Giant panda

Chimpanzee